RYAN EARLEY

MIGHTY TRUCKS

TABLE OF CONTENTS

A Pelican Book

Teaching Tips for Caregivers and Teachers:

Research shows that one of the best ways for students to learn a new topic is to read about it.

Before Reading

- Read the title and predict what the book will be about.
- Read the "Words to Know" and discuss the meaning of each word.
- Read the back cover to see what the book is about.

During Reading

- When a student gets to a word that is unknown, ask them to look at the rest of the sentence to find clues to help with the meaning of the unknown word.
- Motivate students with praise and encouragement.

After Reading

- Discuss the main idea of the book.
- Ask students to give one detail that they learned in the book.

Sight Words

a
all
are
have
is
most
red
some
this

Words to Know

fire truck

hose

ladder

lights

wheels

This is a **fire truck.**

fire truck

Some fire trucks are red.

F.D.
N.Y.
KP15024
KME
4
4

All fire trucks have **wheels**.

380
wheel

Most fire trucks have a **ladder**.

ladder
BRIDGEPORT
FIRE DEPT.
LADDER FIVE
BFD
E-12

All fire trucks have **lights**.

lights
OVERALL HEIGHT 10'-10"
F.D.
N.Y.

All fire trucks have a **hose**.

hose

Index

Written by: Ryan Earley
Design by: Savina Magaro
Editor: Kim Thompson
Series Development: James Earley

Photos: mikeledray: cover; Anne Richard: p. 4-5; Valokuva24: p. 7; BLANKartist: p. 9; Keith Muratori: p. 11; Photo Spirit: p. 13; Tippa Pratt: p. 15

Library of Congress PCN Data
Fire Trucks / Ryan Earley
Mighty Trucks
ISBN 978-1-6389-7949-4(hard cover)
ISBN 979-8-8873-5008-0(paperback)
ISBN 979-8-8873-5067-7(EPUB)
ISBN 979-8-8873-5126-1(eBook)
Library of Congress Control Number: 2022942271
Printed in the United States of America.

Seahorse Publishing Company
seahorsepub.com 1-800-387-7650

Published in the United States
Seahorse Publishing
PO Box 771325
Coral Springs, FL 33077